BIOMIMICRY

AWESOME INNOVATIONS INSPIRED BY SPIDERS

Jim Corrigan

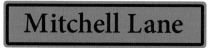

Mitchell Lane

PUBLISHERS

mitchelllane.com

2001 SW 31st Avenue
Hallandale, FL 33009

First Edition, 2021.
Author: Jim Corrigan
Designer: Ed Morgan
Editor: Sharon F. Doorasamy

Series: Biomimicry
Title: Awesome Innovations Inspired by Spiders / by Jim Corrigan

Hallandale, FL : Mitchell Lane Publishers, [2021]

Library bound ISBN: 978-1-68020-611-1
eBook ISBN: 978-1-68020-612-8

Contents

Space Spiders

In July 2012, a rocket launched from Japan. It carried cargo for the International Space Station. The rocket was unmanned, but it had a special passenger. A red-backed jumping spider was on board.

The spider would be part of an experiment. An Egyptian teen named Amr Mohammed had thought of a test. Jumping spiders, he knew, do not build webs. Instead, they simply pounce on their prey.

Amr Mohammed wondered if jumping spiders needed gravity to hunt. Would they still be able to jump in space? His idea, a winner in the YouTube SpaceLab contest, was about to be tested.

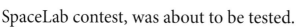

The spider arrived at the space station. Astronauts released some fruit flies into its box. Then they watched and waited.

The astronauts did not need to wait long. The spider spotted its prey. It crept toward an unwary fruit fly, then leapt. In a flash, the jumping spider had caught its first meal in space. It would catch many more flies before returning to Earth.

A Japanese rocket lifts off on July 21, 2012, on its journey to the International Space Station.

Space Explorers

In recent years, space agencies have looked to spiders for more than just experiments. Engineers at NASA (National Aeronautics and Space Administration) are working on a spider robot. They call it Spidernaut. The eight-legged climber will work in the vacuum of space.

Astronauts need bulky suits supplied with heat and air. Spidernaut requires only a battery. It will be able to skitter across solar panels without causing any damage. The robot even has a tether for hanging, just as a real spider hangs from its web.

Engineers in the United Kingdom are building a spider-like rover to explore the moon. Most rovers have wheels, but the tiny Spacebit rover has four spider legs. Its ability to walk and jump will come in handy on the moon's rocky surface.

Spidernaut and the Spacebit rover are **innovations**. The people who invented them were searching for better ways to explore space. Innovators change our world with advances in science and technology.

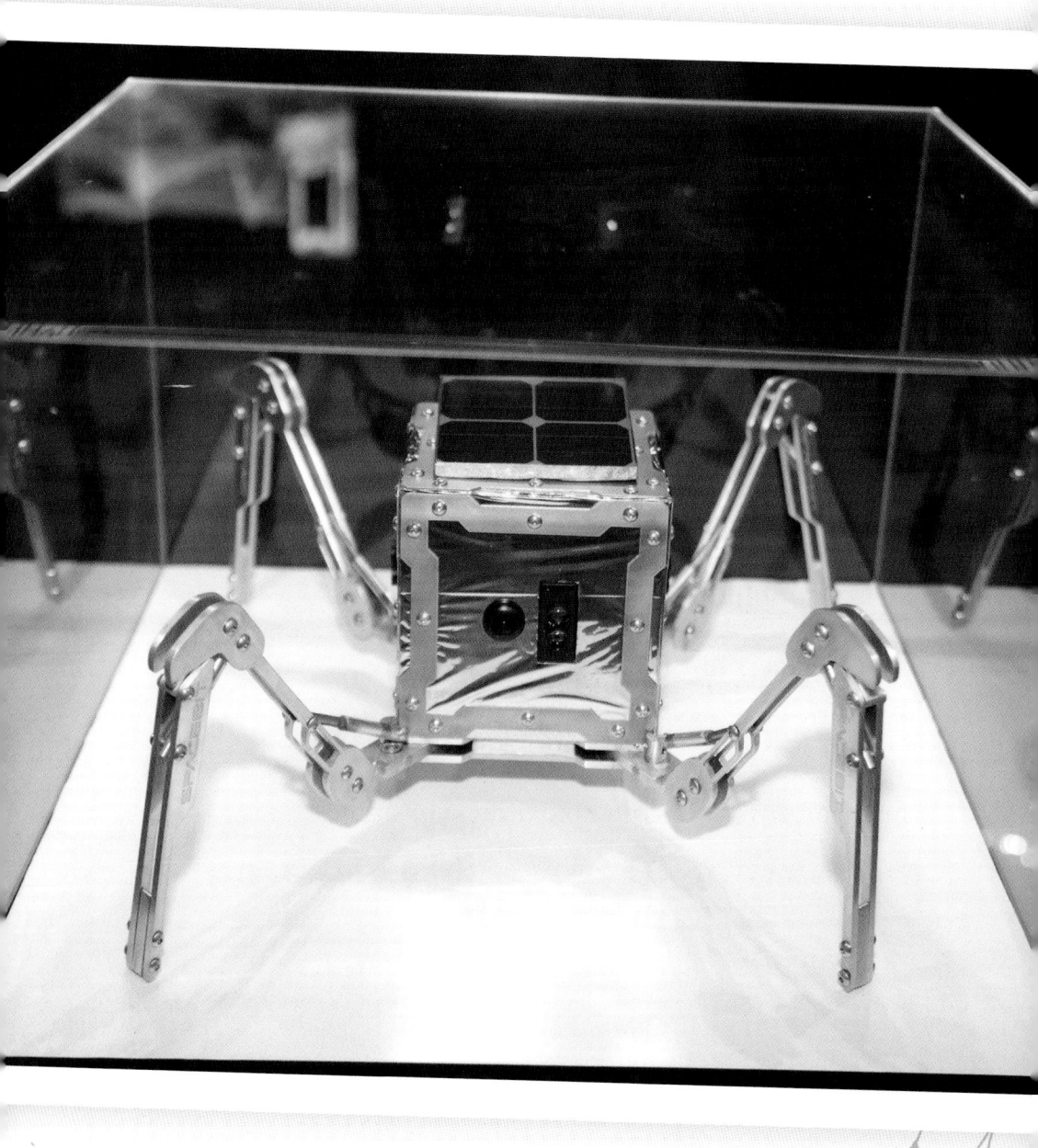

The very small, four-legged Spacebit will move at least 33 feet (10 meters) on the lunar surface and beam high-definition video and other data home during its 10-day mission in July of 2021.

When innovators look to nature for ideas, it is called **biomimicry**. (*Bio* means "life" and *mimic* means "to copy.") Spidernaut and the Spacebit rover are examples of biomimicry. Their creators copied a spider's body to create nimble space robots.

Spiders were around before the dinosaurs. They can be found on every continent except Antarctica. We know of more than 48,000 spider species, with new ones being discovered every year. They offer us many opportunities for biomimicry.

Goldenrod Spider Crabs can change their body color, depending on their environment or the flower on which they are sitting.

You probably have found a few spiders hanging out in your home, but most live outdoors. A single acre of grassy field contains about one million spiders. We need them. Spiders prey on the insects that destroy our food crops. Without spiders, humans would face dire food shortages.

2nd CHAPTER

Silky Secrets

Spiders make silk to build webs and do other tasks. In 2012, a Japanese researcher used spider silk for something remarkable. Shigeyoshi Osaki collected thousands of silk strands from more than 300 spiders. He then spun the strands into a set of violin strings.

Osaki placed his violin strings under a microscope. He found that the silk strands had bonded together perfectly. His spider-silk strings were stronger than traditional nylon strings.

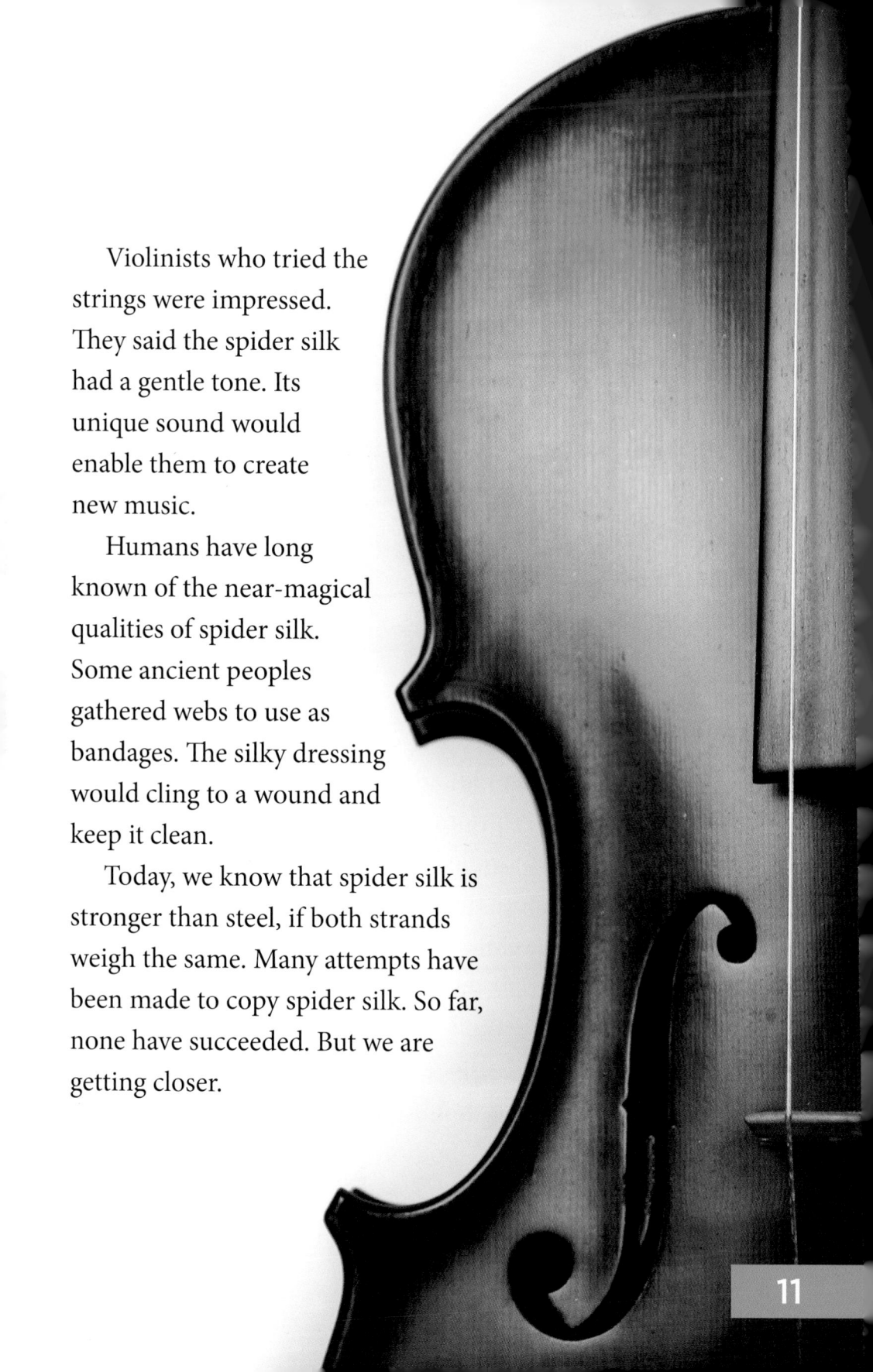

Violinists who tried the strings were impressed. They said the spider silk had a gentle tone. Its unique sound would enable them to create new music.

Humans have long known of the near-magical qualities of spider silk. Some ancient peoples gathered webs to use as bandages. The silky dressing would cling to a wound and keep it clean.

Today, we know that spider silk is stronger than steel, if both strands weigh the same. Many attempts have been made to copy spider silk. So far, none have succeeded. But we are getting closer.

chapter two

An Orb Weaver spider spins silk with its back legs.

How Do They Do It?

Spiders produce silk from glands in their abdomen. Most species can make several different kinds of silk. Dragline silk is strong and ideal for starting a web. Capture-spiral silk is sticky, which is perfect for catching prey. Silk strands come out of a spider through an organ called the **spinneret**.

The American Museum of Natural History in New York has begun building a spider silk "library." So far, museum workers have collected the silk of more than 50 species. They hope to help solve the mysteries of spider silk so we can mimic it.

A strong but lightweight material would have many uses. Airplanes and cars would use less fuel. Soldiers could wear safe but comfortable body armor.

Science writer Janine Benyus notes that biomimicry has an extra benefit. It's safe for the environment. In 1997, Benyus wrote a book entitled *Biomimicry: Innovation Inspired by Nature*. Ever since, she has been urging innovators to find ideas in nature.

The shoe company Adidas believes spider silk is the key to nature-friendly sneakers. Right now, when we throw away an old pair of nylon sneakers, they sit in a landfill for at least 30 years. Cobwebs, however, dissolve much more quickly.

Since 2016, Adidas has been working on a **biodegradable** running shoe. Based on spider silk, the shoe would decay soon after it is discarded.

FUN FACT

Hummingbirds build nests from spider silk, along with twigs and bits of leaves. The nest, which is roughly the size of a golf ball, stretches as the babies grow.

3rd CHAPTER

Web Wonders

Imagine you are a spider.

You have spent all day building a complex web. It is nearly invisible, which is great for catching prey. But if birds cannot see it, your hard work could be ruined in an instant.

Spiders solve this problem with a neat trick. They add special silk strands that reflect **ultraviolet** light. Birds spot these reflectors and dodge the web.

Humans have a bird-collision problem too. Our buildings have windows, which are invisible to birds. Every day worldwide, millions of birds die from flying into windows.

The German company Arnold Glas may have found the answer. It makes an ultraviolet window coating called Ornilux. Birds can see it, but we cannot. In lab tests, 76 percent of birds avoided the Ornilux window. They veered instead toward a traditional glass pane. (A net caught them in time.)

Delightful Décor

Many spiders like to jazz up their webs. Popular decorations include silk spirals and dead leaves. The idea is to lure prey and fool predators.

In Southeast Asia, a silver orb-weaver hides itself as bird poop. The orb-weaver gathers gray leaf bits. It carefully arranges them to look like a bird dropping. Then the spider sits on its web, surrounded by the fake bird poop. Wasps and other predators fly right by.

A rainforest spider in Peru builds a dummy of itself. The spider uses leaf debris and prey corpses to make its look-alike. The decoy has a head, legs, and abdomen. A species in the Philippines does the same thing.

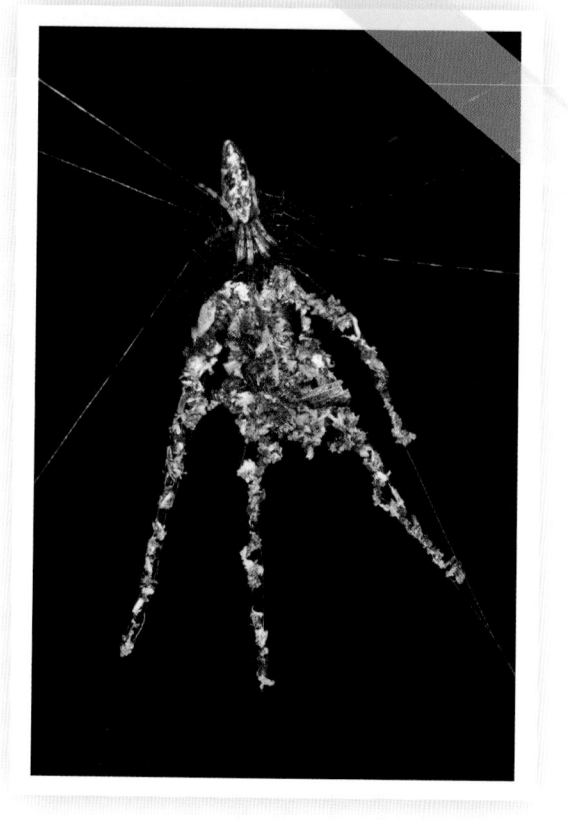

"The Philippine species and the Peruvian species, they both makes these decoys, but the architecture is different," said entomologist Lary Reeves who found the Philippine spider in March 2012.

The Cobweb Bridge is also known as the Spider Bridge.

Designers around the world admire spider webs. In Sheffield, England, a web of slender steel cables supports the Cobweb Bridge. A metal spider hangs above, peering down at bridge walkers.

In Miami, the lobby of the Moore Building features a three-story web sculpture. It clings to pillars overhead.

Architects and engineers study how spider webs resist damage. The stretchy strands can stiffen when necessary. When a strand does break, the rest of the web stays intact. These abilities would be useful for buildings in earthquake zones.

chapter three

Many of us find spiders creepy, but some people panic. Extreme fear of spiders is called **arachnophobia**. In the tropics, where large spiders are common, people have grown used to them. It helps to remember that few species can do us any harm. Spiders try to avoid humans.

Jumping spiders like the one pictured here belong to a large family, with more than 5,800 species. Researchers at the University of Manchester in Great Britain trained a regal jumping spider to jump on command to better understand the species' jumping abilities.

Water Wizards

If you look at a spider with a magnifying glass, you will see lots of hair. Spiders rely on body hair for many key tasks.

Most spiders have eight eyes but poor vision. Tiny hairs offer another way to sense the world. These hairs pick up the slightest vibration. They alert the spider to nearby predators or prey. Some hairs help with tasting food or finding a mate.

Leg hairs enable spiders to climb almost anywhere. The fishing spider, or raft spider, can run across a pond. Its hairy, waxy legs act like the oars of a rowboat.

The fishing spider, also known as the raft spider, can stay under water for up to half an hour!

Soggy hairs would be useless. To avoid this problem, spiders have **water-repellent** hair. A raindrop rolls off its body without making it wet. The hairs have different lengths. Some are straight while others are curved. Water cannot penetrate.

Researchers at the University of Florida have mimicked spider hair. They created a surface that looks flat but has tiny plastic hairs to repel water. Their method, once perfected, will be useful for things like speedboat hulls and nonstick frying pans.

chapter four

Scuba Diver

The diving bell spider is a true water champion. This amazing species spends its life underwater.

On the surface, a diving bell spider traps air between the hairs on its body. Once underwater, the air forms a bubble. The spider then builds a bell-shaped web and anchors it to a plant. This web holds the precious bubble.

With its air supply secure, the spider is free to hunt, mate, and raise its young. In the past, scientists thought diving bell spiders needed to come up for fresh air every 20 minutes. Recent studies have shown that they can stay underwater for an entire day.

Water spiders trap insects and small fish in their bell.

So far, humans have been unable to live underwater for long periods. But that could be changing. Architects at Tokyo's Shimizu Corporation have designed an ocean city. The huge structure would have homes, schools, and labs for 5,000 people.

Water covers about 71 percent of our planet. Oceans offer abundant food and energy. Someday, people might live like the diving bell spider.

FUN FACT

North American tarantulas use spiked hairs for defense. If attacked, the tarantula swipes its hind legs across its back. The rapid motion flings spiky hairs at the attacker.

Spider Sense

Some spiders can fly. They do not have wings, yet they are expert aviators. Their secret is a homemade silk parachute.

On a warm and breezy day, a spider climbs to a treetop or other high spot. It lifts its front legs to sense the air current. The spider then raises its abdomen. Silk strands pour from its spinneret.

The strands form a crude parachute shaped like a triangle. A breeze catches it, lifting the spider into the air, and off it goes. The clever trick is called **ballooning**.

Most flights are shorter than a football field but not all. Some spiders have flown for hundreds of miles. Sailors have reported spiders landing on their ships at sea. In parts of Australia, millions of spiders will balloon at the same time. Afterward, silk parachutes cover the ground like snow.

Recently, scientists have concluded that ballooning spiders use more than just the breeze. They also use Earth's **static electric** field. (Static electricity is what happens to your hair after you rub a balloon on it.) The parachute's negative charge helps propel it into the air.

We are still learning the details of spider flight. Mimicking it might lead to a low-energy method of travel.

chapter five

Valuable Venom

Many spiders kill their prey with venom. Scientists have begun studying the chemical makeup of spider venom. Their hope is to adapt it for human use.

Spiders kill the insects that destroy farm crops. Spider venom is deadly to these pests. In 2018, a company named Vestaron came out with a venom-based **pesticide**. It kills common crop-eaters but does not harm helpful insects, like honeybees.

Huntsman spiders are not dangerous to people. They do possess venom, and a bite can be painful, cause swelling, and even headaches. But these eight-eyed spiders are reluctant to bite and will usually try to run away.

Banana spiders like the one pictured here live in Africa, Asia, Australia, and the southeastern United States, from Texas to North Carolina. They are mildly venomous, causing redness, blisters, and pain at the bite area.

Some medical researchers believe spider venom is the key to better painkillers. Doctors at Yale University and the University of Queensland in Australia are leading the way. They say such drugs could help patients with chronic pain.

Venom and spider silk offer great potential for innovation. Biomimicry is the act of copying nature to solve human problems. Natural solutions do not harm the environment. With biomimicry, people in science and business are finding tomorrow's ideas today.

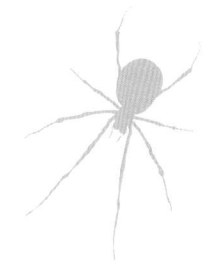

What You
Should Know

Spider silk is stronger than a steel thread of equal weight.

A spider's body hair keeps it dry and helps it sense the surrounding world. Water-repellent materials can be made by mimicking spider hair.

Some spiders fly using a homemade parachute. Other species walk on water. The diving bell spider lives underwater, dragging down air bubbles from the surface.

Spider webs have ultraviolet reflectors so birds can see them. By mimicking this trick, we might keep birds from crashing into glass windows.

The smart ideas that come from biomimicry have an extra benefit. They are safe for the environment.

Want to be an engineer?
Architect? Inventor?

1. Take math and science classes

2. Enroll in art and design classes

3. Attend STEM camps and programs

4. Visit nature preserves and parks to observe nature at work

5. Keep a journal or a blog of your observations

6. Enter science fairs and competitions

7. Check out books on biomimicry from your school and public library

8. Visit natural history museums and science centers

9. Check your community's calendar for talks by science and technology experts

10. Volunteer for citizen science events like bird counts, water sample collection, and weather reporting

Glossary

arachnophobia
An abnormal fear of spiders

ballooning
A method by which some spiders fly to new locations

biodegradable
Capable of decay

biomimicry
Borrowing ideas from nature

innovation
To create or improve an object or method

pesticide
A chemical mix for killing unwanted insects or weeds

spinneret
A spider's organ for dispensing silk

static electricity
An imbalance of electric charges on a material

ultraviolet
A type of light humans cannot see but some other creatures can

water-repellent
Having the ability to resist water

Online Resources

Visit the Conservationist for Kids webpage
www.dec.ny.gov/education/40248.html for more information about:
Biomimicry, Green Chemistry, Green Schools, and Sustainability

Check out the Ask Nature website
www.asknature.org

Listen to Janine Benyus talk about biomimicry
www.ted.com/speakers/janine_benyus

Enjoy the podcast 30 Animals That Made Us Smarter
www.bbc.co.uk/programmes/w13xttw7

Visit the Patents and Trademarks of Biomimicry
www.uspto.gov/kids/Biomimicry.pdf

Learn about different types of spiders and their amazing abilities
https://www.dkfindout.com/uk/animals-and-nature/arachnids/spiders/

Further Reading

Becker, Helaine, and Alex Ries. *Zoobots: Wild Robots Inspired by Real Animals*. Tonawanda, NY: Kids Can Press, 2014.

Bradley, Richard A., and Steve Buchanan. *Common Spiders of North America*. Berkeley, CA: University of California Press, 2019.

Cowles, Jillian. *Amazing Arachnids*. Princeton, NJ: Princeton University Press, 2018.

Koontz, Robin. *Nature-Inspired Contraptions*. North Mankato, MN: Rourke Educational Media, 2018.

Index

About the Author

Jim Corrigan has been writing nonfiction for more than 20 years. He holds degrees from Penn State and Johns Hopkins. Jim became a fan of biomimicry while working on a book about airplanes. He currently lives near Philadelphia.